SCHOLAS

Solve-the-Riddle Math Practice

Time and Money

LIANE B. ONISH

New York • Toronto • London • Auckland • Sydney
Mexico City • New Delhi • Hong Kong • Buenos Aires

Teaching Resources

Hi, Mom!

Thanks, Deborah!

Cover design by Ka-Yeon Kim-Li
Interior design by Holly Grundon
Interior illustrations by Teresa Anderko and Anne Kennedy

ISBN-13: 978-0-545-16327-9
ISBN-10: 0-545-16327-7

Published by Scholastic Inc.

Printed in the U.S.A.
6 7 8 9 10 40 17 16 15 14 13

Contents

About This Book 4

Time:

Analog to Digital

Riddle 1: Telling Time: On the Hour 5

Riddle 2: Telling Time: On the Half Hour 6

Riddle 3: Telling Time: On the Quarter Hour 7

Riddle 4: Mixed Practice 1 (On the Hour, Half Hour, Quarter Hour) 8

Riddle 5: Telling Time: 20-Minute Increments 9

Riddle 6: Telling Time: 10-Minute Increments . . .10

Riddle 7: Telling Time: 5-Minute Increments 11

Riddle 8: Mixed Practice 2 (20-, 10-, 5-Minute Increments) 12

Riddle 9: Elapsed Time: On the Hour 13

Riddle 10: Elapsed Time: On the Half Hour 14

Riddle 11: Elapsed Time: On the Quarter Hour . . .15

Riddle 12: Mixed Practice 3 (Elapsed Time: On the Hour, Half Hour, Quarter Hour) 16

Riddle 13: Elapsed Time: 20-Minute Increments . .17

Riddle 14: Elapsed Time: 10-Minute Increments . .18

Riddle 15: Elapsed Time: 5-Minute Increments . . .19

Riddle 16: Mixed Practice 4 (Elapsed Time: 20-, 10-, 5-Minute Increments) 20

Riddle 17: Time Phrases .21

Riddle 18: Time Phrases .22

Riddle 19: AM and PM 23

Riddle 20: Time Phrases/AM and PM 24

Riddle 21: Mixed Practice 5 (Time Phrases/AM and PM). 25

Riddle 22: Converting Time Units: Hours and Minutes. 26

Riddle 23: Converting Time Units: Hours, Minutes, Seconds 27

Riddle 24: Reading a Schedule 28

Riddle 25: Reading a Schedule 29

Calendar:

Riddle 26: Reading a Calendar 30

Riddle 27: Reading a Calendar 31

Riddle 28: Converting Calendar Units 32

Riddle 29: Mixed Practice 6 (Calendar Concepts) .33

Money:

Riddle 30: Adding Coin Values to 50¢ 34

Riddle 31: Computing Prices to 50¢ 35

Riddle 32: Finding Missing Coin Values to 50¢ . . .36

Riddle 33: Making Change From 50¢ 37

Riddle 34: Mixed Practice 7 (Values to 50¢) 38

Riddle 35: Adding Coin Values to $1.00. 39

Riddle 36: Computing Prices to $1.00 40

Riddle 37: Finding Missing Coin Values to $1.00 .41

Riddle 38: Making Change From $1.00 42

Riddle 39: Mixed Practice 8 (Values to $1.00) . . .43

Riddle 40: Adding Coin and Dollar Values to $2.00 44

Riddle 41: Computing Prices to $2.00 45

Riddle 42: Finding Missing Money Values to $2.00 46

Riddle 43: Making Change From $2.00 47

Riddle 44: Mixed Practice 9 (Values to $2.00) 48

Riddle 45: Adding Money Values to $5.00 49

Riddle 46: Computing Prices to $5.00 50

Riddle 47: Finding Missing Money Values to $5.00 51

Riddle 48: Making Change From $5.00 52

Riddle 49: Mixed Practice 10 (Values to $5.00) . . .53

Riddle 50: Adding Money Values to $10.00 54

Riddle 51: Computing Prices to $10.00 55

Riddle 52: Finding Missing Money Values to $10.00 56

Riddle 53: Making Change From $10.00 57

Riddle 54: Mixed Practice 11 (Values to $10.00) . .58

Riddle 55: Estimating Prices 59

Riddle 56: Estimating Prices 60

Riddle 57: Estimating Prices. 61

Answer Key 62

About This Book

Research shows that to master math skills, students need plenty of sustained practice. Understanding time concepts and working with money are essential skills for success in math and in life. The silly riddles on the activity pages in this book will motivate students to complete the math problems and get this needed practice. Each answer is keyed to a letter. Located below the math problems is the solution to the riddle. Students write the letter that corresponds to each numerical answer to spell out the solution to the riddle. Voila! Math practiced, riddle solved!

Meeting the Math Standards

The National Council of Teachers of Mathematics (NCTM) has outlined learning expectations and focal points—key concepts and skills for emphasis at different grade levels. The activities in this book align with the Measurement, Problem Solving, and Number and Operations standards for grades 2 and 3 (nctm.org/standards).

For an overview of specific math skills covered in this book, see the Contents page. (These math skills are also listed at the top of each activity sheet.) Activity pages 5-33 (Riddles 1-29) focus on skills and concepts involving time. Pages 34-61 (Riddles 30-57) focus on concepts involving money. Use your students' different ability levels as a guide when assigning the activity sheets.

Introducing the Activities

Read the riddle and math directions with students. Point out the letter below or next to each answer's write-on line. Explain that the answers have the letters students will use to solve the riddle. After they complete the math, direct them to the bottom of the page. Have them read the number under the solution's first write-on line, then find that number in their math answers. Instruct them to write the letter that goes with that number answer on the line. When all of the letters have been filled in, invite students to reread the riddle and the solution. Discuss the word play in the riddles, which rely mostly on multiple meaning and puns.

Extra Practice Challenge

Invite students to create their own time and money practice pages for their favorite riddles. Remind them that for an activity with twelve problems, the answer to the riddle can be no more than twelve different letters of the alphabet. Have students write a letter below the answer for each problem. Then have them check their work and write an answer key on a separate sheet of paper. Collect the student-made activity pages, mix them up, and distribute randomly.

Math Vocabulary Teaching Tip

Review math vocabulary for time-related terms, such as *hour, half hour, minute, second, before/after, earlier/later, o'clock, AM/PM, half past, a quarter to; day, week, month, year.* Review money-related terms as well, including *cent, penny, nickel, dime, quarter, dollar, cost, value, left, change,* and *estimate.* The mathematical symbols used in writing about time and money—colons (:) to separate hours from minutes; and cents (¢), dollars ($), and decimal points (.) to separate dollars and cents—should also be discussed. Explain to students that amounts less than one dollar may be expressed in two different ways, for example, 27¢ and $.27. A review of these math terms will be especially helpful to English language learners.

Name: ______________________ Date: ____________

Riddle 1

What wakes the dragon each morning?

Read the clocks. Write the times.
Solve the riddle using your answers below.

___:___ L	___:___ D	___:___ F
___:___ E	___:___ I	___:___ M
___:___ R	___:___ A	___:___ B

Solve the Riddle! Write the letter that goes with each time.

___ 9:00   ___ 10:00   ___ 2:00   ___ 6:00   ___ 11:00

___ 9:00   ___ 5:00   ___ 9:00   ___ 6:00   ___ 8:00

Name: ______________________ Date: __________

Riddle 2

What is a frog's favorite snack?

Read the clocks. Write the times.
Solve the riddle using your answers below.

 ___ : ___ O	 ___ : ___ B	 ___ : ___ A
 ___ : ___ K	 ___ : ___ E	 ___ : ___ C
 ___ : ___ J	 ___ : ___ R	 ___ : ___ S

Solve the Riddle! Write the letter that goes with each time.

___ 7:30 ___ 12:30 ___ 4:30 ___ 2:30 ___ 6:30 ___ 9:30 ___ 12:30

___ 1:30 ___ 2:30 ___ 7:30 ___ 6:30 ___ 3:30

Name: ____________________ Date: ____________

Riddle 3

What do Martians roast over campfires?

Read the clocks. Write the times.
Solve the riddle using your answers below.

___ : ___ A	___ : ___ B	___ : ___ M
___ : ___ R	___ : ___ L	___ : ___ O
___ : ___ W	___ : ___ S	___ : ___ E

Solve the Riddle! Write the letter that goes with each time.

___	___	___	___	–	___	___	___	___	___	___	___
1:15	2:15	6:45	12:45		1:15	2:15	10:15	10:15	4:45	9:15	12:45

Name: ____________________ Date: ____________

Riddle 4

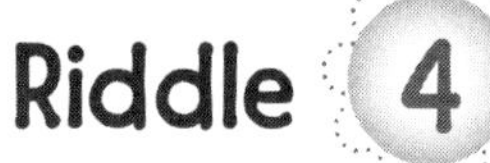

What is the meanest farm animal?

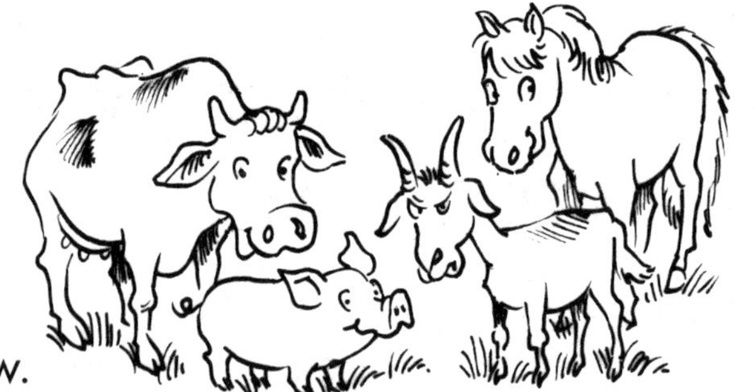

Read the clocks. Write the times.
Solve the riddle using your answers below.

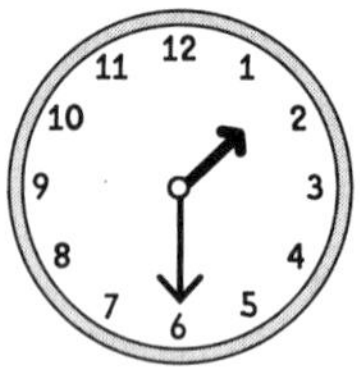 ___:___ L	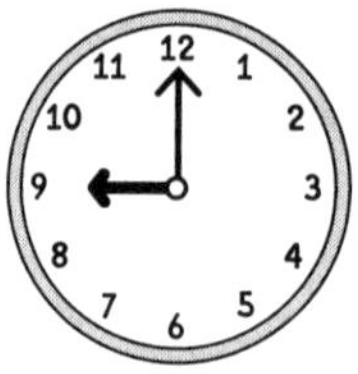 ___:___ B	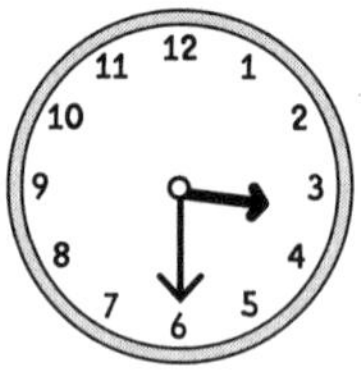 ___:___ G
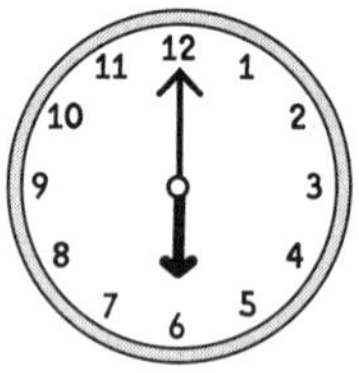 ___:___ T	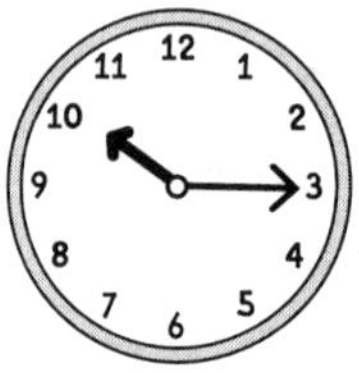 ___:___ A	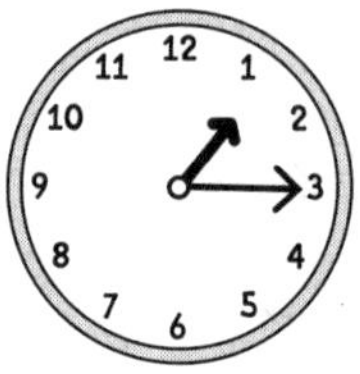 ___:___ U
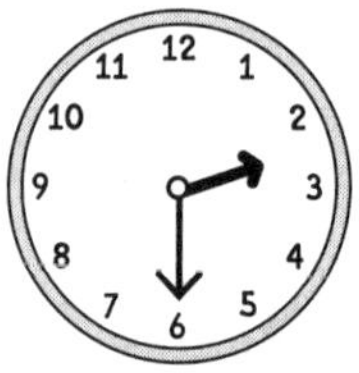 ___:___ O	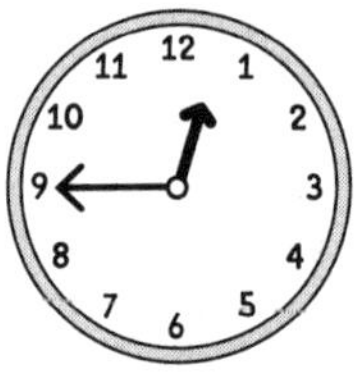 ___:___ Y	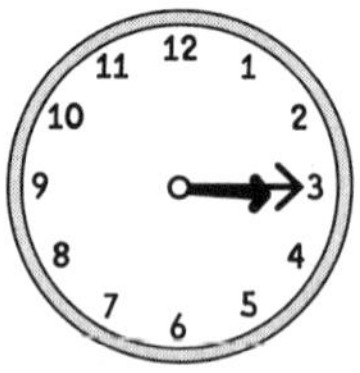 ___:___ R

Solve the Riddle! Write the letter that goes with each time.

___ 10:15 ___ 9:00 ___ 1:15 ___ 1:30 ___ 1:30 ___ 12:45 ___ 3:30 ___ 2:30 ___ 10:15 ___ 6:00

Name: ______________________ Date: ____________

Riddle 5

What do you call angry cats?

Read the clocks. Write the times.
Solve the riddle using your answers below.

___:___ S	___:___ U	___:___ E
___:___ F	___:___ A	___:___ I
___:___ R	___:___ T	___:___ O

Solve the Riddle! Write the letter that goes with each time.

___ ___ ___ - ___ ___ ___ ___
1:40 7:40 9:20 4:20 12:40 7:40 3:20

Name: ______________________ Date: ____________

Riddle 6

What will the head fly do when the others won't work?

Read the clocks. Write the times.
Solve the riddle using your answers below.

___:___ L	___:___ E	___:___ H
___:___ N	___:___ F	___:___ S
___:___ R	___:___ T	___:___ I

Solve the Riddle! Write the letter that goes with each time.

___ ___ ___ ___   ___ ___ ___ ___ ___
7:40 10:40 4:10 5:20   7:40 9:10 10:40 5:20 11:10

Name: ______________________ Date: ____________

Riddle 

What did the dog say when he stubbed his paw?

Read the clocks. Write the times.
Solve the riddle using your answers below.

 ___:___ O	 ___:___ F	 ___:___ T
 ___:___ S	 ___:___ L	 ___:___ E
 ___:___ N	 ___:___ W	 ___:___ I

Solve the Riddle! Write the letter that goes with each time.

___ ___ – ___ ___ ___ !
5:05 10:45 10:45 5:05 10:45

Name: ______________________ Date: ______________

Riddle 8

What does Pinocchio feed his wooden dog?

Read the clocks. Write the times.
Solve the riddle using your answers below.

___:___ C	___:___ P	___:___ U
___:___ W	___:___ F	___:___ T
___:___ H	___:___ E	___:___ O

Solve the Riddle! Write the letter that goes with each time.

___	___	___	___	___	___		___	___	___	___
10:35	7:05	10:35	10:35	3:20	5:50		2:25	4:50	9:40	8:10

Name: ______________________ Date: ______________

Riddle 9

What does the caterpillar crossing guard say?

Read the clocks. Write the times.
Solve the riddle using your answers below.

The time is ___:___ B

One hour earlier is ___:___ K

Two hours later is ___:___ F

The time is ___:___ Y

Two hours earlier is ___:___ S

Four hours later is ___:___ L

The time is ___:___ R

Three hours earlier is ___:___ C

One hour later is ___:___ O

The time is ___:___ U

Three hours earlier is ___:___ P

Five hours later is ___:___ E

Solve the Riddle! Write the letter that goes with each time.

___ ___ ___ ___   ___ ___ ___ ___ ___ ___
9:00 8:00 8:00 11:00   12:00 6:00 2:00 8:00 7:00 6:00

___ ___ ___   ___ ___ ___ ___ ___ .
5:00 8:00 1:00   4:00 7:00 6:00 6:00 10:00

Name: ____________________ Date: ____________

Riddle 10

What game do bees like to play?

Read the clocks. Write the times.
Solve the riddle using your answers below.

The time is ___:___ A

one half hour earlier is ___:___ H

three hours later is ___:___ N

The time is ___:___ I

six and one half hours earlier is ___:___ S

seven hours later is ___:___ E

The time is ___:___ V

five hours earlier is ___:___ B

two and one half hours later is ___:___ F

The time is ___:___ D

one and one half hours earlier is ___:___ R

one half hour later is ___:___ K

Solve the Riddle! Write the letter that goes with each time.

___ ___ ___ ___ – ___ ___ ___ – ___ ___ ___ ___ !

2:00 6:30 12:30 1:30 – 2:30 5:30 10:30 – 12:00 1:30 1:30 11:00

Name: ______________________ Date: ____________

Riddle 11

What's another name for lovebirds?

Read the clocks. Write the times.
Solve the riddle using your answers below.

The time is ___:___ D

A quarter hour earlier is ___:___ N

A quarter hour later is ___:___ E

The time is ___:___ H

A quarter hour earlier is ___:___ R

A quarter hour later is ___:___ V

The time is ___:___ W

A quarter hour earlier is ___:___ M

A quarter hour later is ___:___ S

The time is ___:___ N

A quarter hour earlier is ___:___ T

A quarter hour later is ___:___ A

Solve the Riddle! Write the letter that goes with each time.

___	___	___	___	___	–	___	___	___	___	___	___
10:00	4:45	1:30	1:30	10:00		7:45	1:30	10:30	7:30	10:00	5:00

Name: ____________________ Date: __________

Riddle 12

Who won first prize at the weightlifting contest?

Read the clocks. Write the times.
Solve the riddle using your answers below.

The time is ___:___ E

$\frac{1}{2}$ hour earlier is ___:___ N

$\frac{1}{4}$ hour later is ___:___ D

The time is ___:___ I

1 hour earlier is ___:___ L

2 hours later is ___:___ W

The time is ___:___ T

1 hour earlier is ___:___ U

$\frac{1}{2}$ hour later is ___:___ R

The time is ___:___ S

$\frac{1}{4}$ hour earlier is ___:___ H

$2\frac{1}{2}$ hours later is ___:___ M

Solve the Riddle! Write the letter that goes with each time.

___ ___ ___   ___ ___ ___   ___ ___ ___
7:30 3:15 1:30   11:30 9:30 1:00   1:00 1:30 8:00

Name: ____________________ Date: __________

Riddle 13

Which ocean won the race?

Read the clocks. Write the times.
Solve the riddle using your answers below.

The time is ___:___ E

20 minutes earlier is ___:___ T

20 minutes later is ___:___ L

The time is ___:___ P

20 minutes earlier is ___:___ C

20 minutes later is ___:___ I

The time is ___:___ A

20 minutes earlier is ___:___ D

20 minutes later is ___:___ Y

The time is ___:___ M

20 minutes earlier is ___:___ H

20 minutes later is ___:___ J

Solve the Riddle! Write the letter that goes with each time.

___	___	___	___		___	___	___	___ .
1:00	11:20	1:20	4:50		1:00	7:20	4:10	1:20

Name: ____________________ Date: __________

Riddle 14

How do you make an eggroll?

Read the clocks. Write the times.
Solve the riddle using your answers below.

The time is ___:___ H

10 minutes earlier is ___:___ A

10 minutes later is ___:___ U

The time is ___:___ W

10 minutes earlier is ___:___ P

10 minutes later is ___:___ E

The time is ___:___ T

10 minutes earlier is ___:___ F

10 minutes later is ___:___ I

The time is ___:___ S

10 minutes earlier is ___:___ R

10 minutes later is ___:___ N

Solve the Riddle! Write the letter that goes with each time.

___ ___ ___ ___   ___ ___ .

8:20 2:50 10:50 2:40   5:20 5:10

Name: ______________________ Date: ____________

What is a wolf's favorite holiday?

Read the clocks. Write the times.
Solve the riddle using your answers below.

 The time is ___:___ E 5 minutes earlier is ___:___ W 5 minutes later is ___:___ T	 The time is ___:___ A 5 minutes earlier is ___:___ H 5 minutes later is ___:___ S
 The time is ___:___ J 5 minutes earlier is ___:___ O 5 minutes later is ___:___ C	 The time is ___:___ N 5 minutes earlier is ___:___ R 5 minutes later is ___:___ L

Solve the Riddle! Write the letter that goes with each time.

___	___	___	___	-	___	___	___	___	___
9:15	6:05	1:25	11:20		6:05	1:25	1:30	1:30	11:15

Name: ______________________ Date: ____________

Riddle 16

What cup won't hold water?

Read the clocks. Write the times.
Solve the riddle using your answers below.

The time is ___:___ U

20 minutes earlier is ___:___ G

5 minutes later is ___:___ B

The time is ___:___ C

5 minutes earlier is ___:___ N

10 minutes later is ___:___ E

The time is ___:___ A

10 minutes earlier is ___:___ W

10 minutes later is ___:___ P

The time is ___:___ K

10 minutes earlier is ___:___ R

10 minutes later is ___:___ I

Solve the Riddle! Write the letter that goes with each time.

___ ___ ___ ___ ___ ___ ___ ___
8:30 3:00 2:30 8:40 3:00 8:30 12:20 3:10

Name: ______________________ Date: ____________

Riddle 17

In what kind of story do the BAD guys live happily ever after?

Write the times. Solve the riddle using your answers below.

five minutes after four o'clock	___:___ A	twenty minutes before 12:00	___:___ U
fifteen minutes before two o'clock	___:___ Y	five minutes after 6:30	___:___ I
ten minutes after nine o'clock	___:___ F	fifteen minutes before 3:00	___:___ R
twenty minutes before six o'clock	___:___ T	twenty minutes after 7:20	___:___ D
thirty minutes after one o'clock	___:___ S	thirty minutes before 5:00	___:___ E
five minutes before three o'clock	___:___ L	forty-five minutes after 12:00	___:___ N

Solve the Riddle! Write the letter that goes with each time.

___ ___   ___ ___ ___ ___ ___ ___ - ___
4:05 12:45   11:40 12:45 9:10 4:05 6:35 2:45 1:45

___ ___ ___ ___
5:40 4:05 2:55 4:30

Name: ______________________ Date: ____________

Riddle 18

What is the world's biggest ant?

Write the time. Solve the riddle using your answers below.

a quarter to seven o'clock ___:___ A	ten minutes before eight o'clock ___:___ P
half past three ___:___ R	five minutes after eleven o'clock ___:___ E
a quarter past nine o'clock ___:___ T	fifteen minutes before three o'clock ___:___ N
twenty minutes before six o'clock ___:___ L	three quarters of an hour past noon ___:___ H
a quarter past one o'clock ___:___ S	twenty-five minutes to five ___:___ W

Solve the Riddle! Write the letter that goes with each time.

___	___	___	___	___	–	___	___	___
11:05	5:40	11:05	7:50	12:45		6:45	2:45	9:15

Time:
AM and PM

Name: ______________________ Date: ______________

Riddle 19

What kind of cookie do termites like best?

Circle the time that makes the most sense.
Solve the riddle using your answers below.

My alarm clock rings in the morning at	I get home from school at
7:15 AM (A) — 7:15 PM (D)	3:30 AM (C) — 3:30 PM (M)
I do my homework at	We eat lunch at
5:00 AM (H) — 5:00 PM (N)	12:10 AM (B) — 12:10 PM (E)
The sun rises at	Mom had an early meeting at
5:45 AM (O) — 5:45 PM (R)	7:00 AM (L) — 7:00 PM (Y)
I go to bed at	Our class meeting is at
8:30 AM (U) — 8:30 PM (T)	9:10 AM (K) — 9:10 PM (I)

Solve the Riddle! Write the letter that goes with each time.

___ ___ ___ - ___ ___ ___ ___
5:45 AM 7:15 AM 9:10 AM 3:30 PM 12:10 PM 7:15 AM 7:00 AM

Name: ______________________ Date: ____________

Riddle 20

What duet do police officers play on the piano?

Write the time. Circle AM or PM. Solve the riddle using your answers below.

half past noon ___ : ___ AM or PM P	a quarter to four in the morning ___ : ___ AM or PM F
ten after nine in the morning ___ : ___ AM or PM N	twenty minutes to two in the morning ___ : ___ AM or PM C
Fifteen after eleven in the morning ___ : ___ AM or PM T	three quarters of an hour after three in the afternoon ___ : ___ AM or PM I
fifty minutes before ten at night ___ : ___ AM or PM O	half past midnight ___ : ___ AM or PM B
twenty minutes to two in the afternoon ___ : ___ AM or PM K	forty-five minutes before midnight ___ : ___ AM or PM S

Solve the Riddle! Write the letter that goes with each time.

___ 1:40 AM ___ 9:10 PM ___ 12:30 PM

___ 11:15 PM ___ 11:15 AM ___ 3:45 PM ___ 1:40 AM ___ 1:40 PM ___ 11:15 PM

Name: ______________________ Date: ____________

Riddle 21

What's the difference between a pear and a pearl?

Write or circle the correct time. Solve the riddle using your answers below.

ten minutes to eight o'clock ___:___ P	five minutes before three o'clock ___:___ T
a quarter past four ___:___ E	half past five ___:___ O
twenty minutes after six o'clock ___:___ F	half an hour before one o'clock ___:___ A
Lila's 6th birthday party starts at 1:00 AM (J) 1:00 PM (H)	We woke up to go fishing at 4:30 AM (D) 4:30 PM (I)
The after-school activities start at 3:30 AM (B) 3:30 PM (R)	They had breakfast at 7:15 AM (L) 7:15 PM (S)

Solve the Riddle! Write the letter that goes with each time.

___ ___ ___
2:55 1:00 PM 4:15

___ ___ ___ ___ ___ ___ ___
7:15 AM 4:15 2:55 2:55 4:15 3:30 PM 7:15 AM

Name: ____________________ Date: __________

Riddle 22

What kind of birds are the silliest?

Convert the time units.
Solve the riddle using your answers below.

1 hour = 60 minutes

1 hour + 1 hour = ______ minutes B	2 hours – 1 hour = ______ minutes O
1 hour + 5 minutes = ______ minutes R	1 hour – 20 minutes = ______ minutes S
1 hour + 1 half hour = ______ minutes A	1 hour – 1 half hour = ______ minutes J
2 hours + 20 minutes = ______ minutes E	1 half hour – 15 minutes = ______ minutes K
$1\frac{1}{2}$ hours + 10 minutes = ______ minutes T	1 quarter hour – 5 minutes = ______ minutes Y

Solve the Riddle! Write the letter that goes with each number.

___ ___ ___ ___ - ___ ___ ___ ___ ___
15 60 60 15 90 100 60 60 40

Name: ______________________ Date: ____________

Riddle 23

What do you call a dentist who will clean an alligator's teeth?

1 hour = 60 minutes
1 minute = 60 seconds

Convert the time units.
Solve the riddle using your answers below.

1 hour + 20 minutes = _____ minutes (Z)	2 minutes = _____ seconds (E)
2 hours + 10 minutes = _____ minutes (D)	half a minute = _____ seconds (R)
2 hours – 20 minutes = _____ minutes (Y)	$1\frac{1}{2}$ minutes = _____ seconds (M)
1 hour – 50 minutes = _____ minutes (C)	1 minute + 15 seconds = _____ seconds (L)
1 hour – 15 minutes = _____ minutes (O)	1 minute – 10 seconds = _____ seconds (A)

Solve the Riddle! Write the letter that goes with each number.

___ ___ ___ ___ ___ !
10 30 50 80 100

Name: ______________________ Date: ____________

Riddle 24

What sport do dogs like best?

Use the schedule to answer the questions.
Solve the riddle using your answers below.

Fun Park Trolley Station			
Trolley	TO	DEPARTS	ARRIVES
#4	Roller Coaster	1:10	1:20
#7	Petting Zoo	2:30	3:00
#12	Ferris Wheel	4:40	4:55
#28	Video Arcade	5:50	6:25

Which trolley goes to the Petting Zoo? #_____ U	How long is the trip to the Roller Coaster? _____ minutes B
How long is the trip to the Petting Zoo? _____ minutes A	Which trolley has the shortest trip? #_____ S
Which trolley goes to the Ferris Wheel? #_____ I	Which trolley has the longest trip? #_____ L
How much shorter is the trip to the Ferris Wheel than to the Petting Zoo? _____ minutes C	How much longer is the trip to the Video Arcade than to the Roller Coaster? _____ minutes T

Solve the Riddle! Write the letter that goes with each number.

___ ___ ___ ___ ___ ___ ___   ___ ___ ___ ___
10 12 4 15 7 12 25   10 30 28 28

Name: ______________________ Date: __________

Riddle 25

Where do impolite cowboys ride horses?

Use the schedule to answer the questions. Solve the riddle using your answers below.

Jill's Gym Workout	
Warm-up	9:15
Yoga	9:30
Swim	10:00
Lift weights	10:45
Run on treadmill	11:00

When does Jill begin her warm-up? ______ D	How much time does Jill spend swimming? ______ minutes A
How long is Jill's yoga class? ______ minutes O	How much longer does Jill swim than do yoga? ______ minutes U
At what time does Jill run on the treadmill? ______ R	How much time does Jill spend doing her warm-up and swimming? ______ minutes E

Solve the Riddle! Write the letter that goes with each number or time.

___ ___ ___ ___ ___ - ___ ___
45 11:00 15 9:45 60 60 30

Name: ____________________ Date: ____________

Riddle 26

What did one volcano say to the other?

Use the calendar to answer the questions.
Solve the riddle using your answers below.

November						
SUN	MON	TUE	WED	THU	FRI	SAT
		1	2	3	4	5
6	7	8	9	10	11	12
13	14	15	16	17	18	19
20	21	22	23	24 Thanksgiving	25	26
27	28	29	30			

Number of days in November ______ A	The fourth Monday is November ______ th. L
Number of full weeks ______ Y	Thanksgiving is on November ______ th. E
Number of Wednesdays ______ I	The Thursday before Thanksgiving is November ______ th. V
The second Friday is November ______ th. O	The Saturday after November 12 is November ______ th. U

Solve the Riddle! Write the letter that goes with each number.

___   ___ ___ ___ ___   ___ ___ ___ .
5   28 30 17 30   3 11 19

Name: ______________________ Date: ____________

Riddle 27

What state has cows in it?

Use the calendar to answer the questions.
Solve the riddle using your answers below.

July						
SUN	MON	TUE	WED	THU	FRI	SAT
				1	2	3
4 Independence Day	5	6	7	8	9	10
11	12	13	14	15	16	17
18	19	20	21	22	23	24
25	26	27	28	29	30	31

How many Saturdays are in July? ______ O	The Thursday after Independence Day is the ______ th. S
Ten days after Independence Day is July ______ th. P	The third Sunday after Independence Day is the ______ th. I
A week after Independence Day is the ______ th. A	The fourth Friday in July is the ______ rd. M
Two weeks after Independence Day is the ______ th. R	The last Thursday in July is the ______ th. U

Solve the Riddle! Write the letter that goes with each number.

___ ___ ___ - ___ ___ ___ ___ ___
23 5 5 8 5 29 18 25

Name: ____________________ Date: __________

Riddle 28

What metal do robbers like best?

Use the poem to answer the questions.
Solve the riddle using your answers below.

> 30 days has September,
> April, June, and November.
> All the rest have 31,
> Except for February. (It has 28 days.)

January + December = ______ days (E)	March + April = ______ days (T)
April + November = _____ days (R)	January + June + July = ______ days (I)
February + April = _____ days (S)	September + October + November = ______ days (O)
January + February = ______ days (N)	May + August + December = ______ days (L)

Solve the Riddle! Write the letter that goes with each number.

___ ___ ___ ___ ___
58 61 62 62 93

Name: ______________________ Date: ____________

Riddle 29

What do bees wear to the beach?

Convert the calendar units.
Solve the riddle using your answers below.

1 day = 24 hours	1 year = 12 months
1 week = 7 days	1 year = 52 weeks

2 days = ______ hours (B)	half a year = ______ weeks (N)
half a day = ______ hours (S)	2 years = ______ weeks (I)
2 weeks = ______ days (K)	half a year = ______ months (E)
3 weeks = ______ days (M)	2 years = ______ months (T)

Solve the Riddle! Write the letter that goes with each number.

___ ___ ___ - ___ ___ ___ ___ ___
48 6 6 14 104 26 104 12

Name: ______________________ Date: ____________

Riddle 30

What starts with *e*, ends with *e*, and has one letter in it?

Find the value of the coins.
Solve the riddle using your answers below.

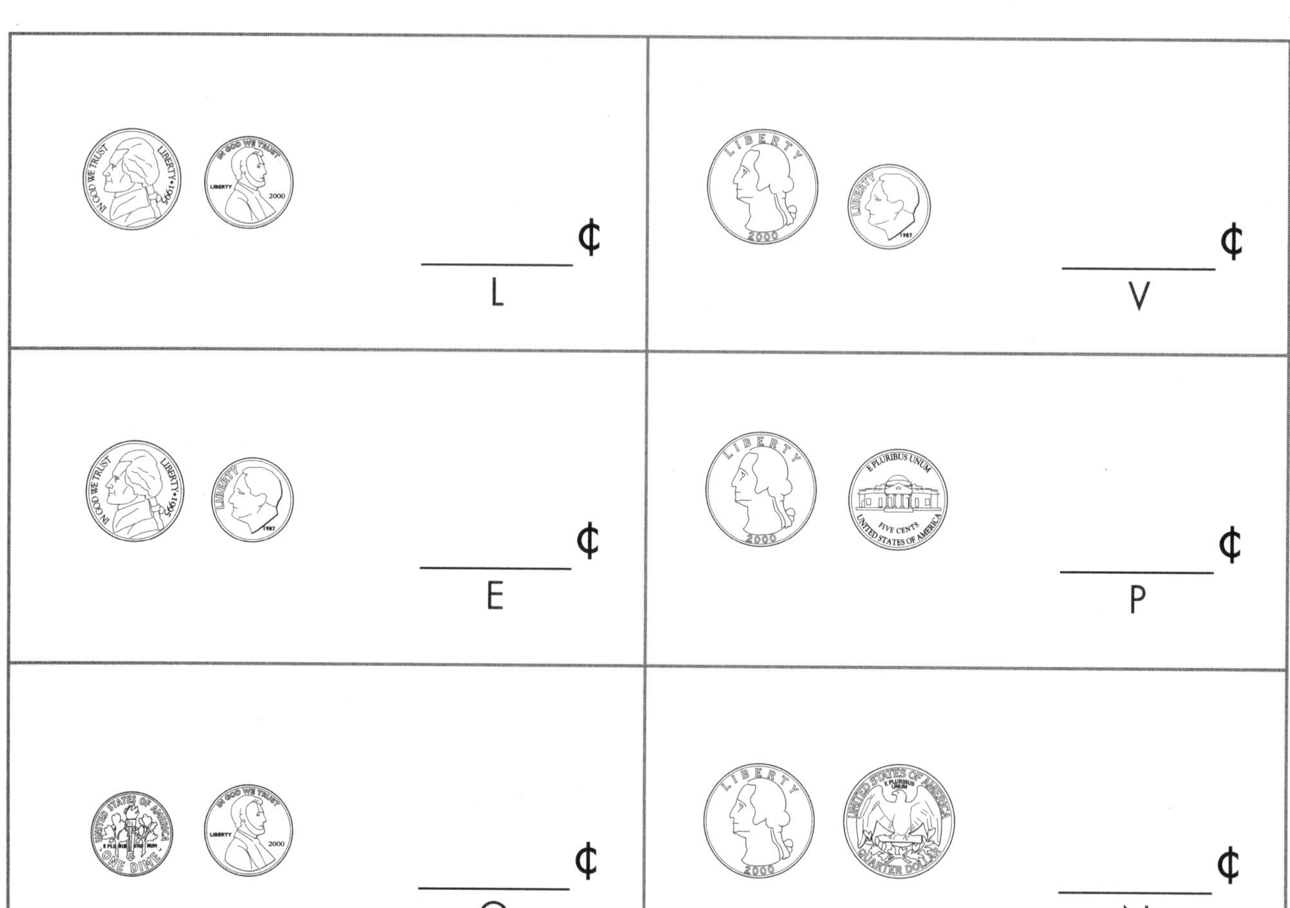

Solve the Riddle! Write the letter that goes with each value.

___	___	___	___	___	___	___	___
15¢	50¢	35¢	15¢	6¢	11¢	30¢	15¢

Name: ______________________ Date: ____________

Riddle 31

What is a bee's favorite vegetable?

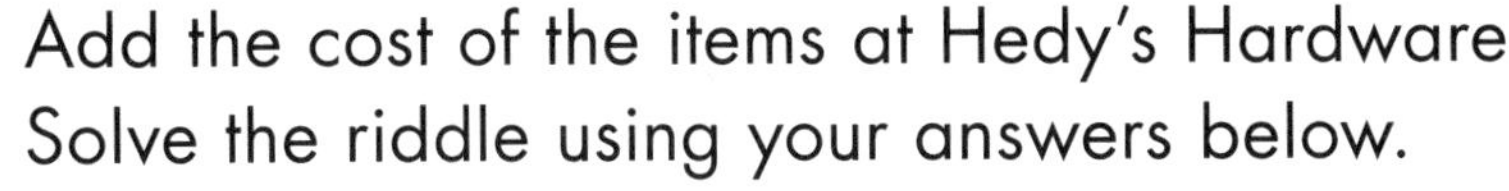

Add the cost of the items at Hedy's Hardware. Solve the riddle using your answers below.

Hedy's Hardware		
hook . . . . . 15¢ bolt . . . . . . 10¢	short nail . . . 4 ¢ drill bit . . . . 25¢	long nail . . . . 8¢ screw . . . . 12¢

2 screws cost ________¢ B	2 bolts and 2 short nails cost ________¢ T
1 hook and 1 drill bit cost ________¢ I	1 drill bit, 1 hook, and 1 bolt cost ________¢ G
3 short nails and 3 long nails cost ________¢ S	1 long nail and 1 drill bit cost ________¢ E
How many drill bits can you buy with 50¢? ________ A	How many hooks can you buy with 45¢? ________ N

Solve the Riddle! Write the letter that goes with each number or value.

___	___	___	___	___		___	___	___	___	___
36¢	28¢	40¢	3	50¢		24¢	33¢	2	3	36¢

Name: ______________________ Date: ____________

Riddle 32

What flowers do ballerinas like best?

Add the coin values.
How much more do you need to make 50¢?
Solve the riddle using your answers below.

+ + ______¢ = 50¢ U	+ + ______¢ = 50¢ I
 + + ______¢ = 50¢ S	+ + ______¢ = 50¢ R
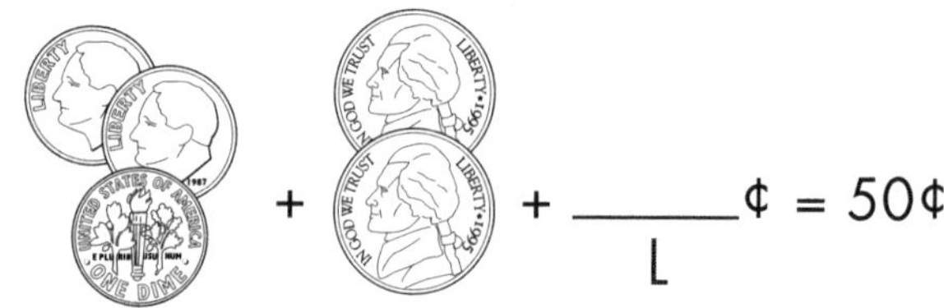 + + ______¢ = 50¢ L	+ + ______¢ = 50¢ P
 + + ______¢ = 50¢ O	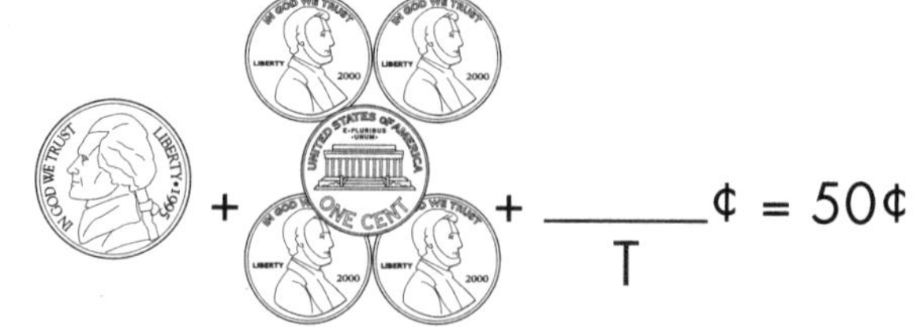 + + ______¢ = 50¢ T

Solve the Riddle! Write the letter that goes with each value.

___ ___ ___ ___ - ___ ___ ___ ___
40¢ 15¢ 40¢ 15¢ 10¢ 25¢ 5¢ 20¢

Name: ______________________ Date: ____________

Riddle 33

How long is a pair of shoes?

Make change from 50¢.
Solve the riddle using your answers below.

You spend 40¢. You have ______¢ left. O	You spend 11¢. You have ______¢ left. R
You spend 39¢. You have ______¢ left. E	You spend 23¢. You have ______¢ left. W
You spend 15¢. You have ______¢ left. K	You spend 10¢. You have ______¢ left. L
You spend 27¢. You have ______¢ left. Y	You spend 34¢. You have ______¢ left. F
You spend 48¢. You have ______¢ left. H	You spend 17¢. You have ______¢ left. B
You spend 7¢. You have ______¢ left. T	You spend 31¢. You have ______¢ left. J

Solve the Riddle! Write the letter that goes with each value.

___ ___ ___   ___ ___ ___ ___
43¢ 27¢ 10¢   16¢ 11¢ 11¢ 43¢

Name: ______________________ Date: __________

Riddle 34

What is the healthiest water?

Find the answers to the problems.
Solve the riddle using your answers below.

 = _____¢ E	= _____¢ P
You have 50¢. You spend 4¢. You have _____¢ left. T	You have 50¢. You spend 32¢. You have _____¢ left. H
What do you need to make 50¢?  + + _____¢ = 50¢ A	What do you need to make 50¢?  + + _____¢ = 50¢ W
How much do 3 apples cost? _____¢ L	How many cookies can you buy with 50¢? _____ R

Solve the Riddle! Write the letter that goes with each number or value.

___	___	___	___		___	___	___	___	___
15¢	25¢	45¢	45¢		15¢	20¢	46¢	25¢	5

Name: ____________________ Date: ____________

Riddle 35

What dance do Australian animals like best?

Add the coin values.
Solve the riddle using your answers below.

______¢ A	______¢ O
______¢ R	______¢ N
______¢ G	______¢ T

Solve the Riddle! Write the letter that goes with each value.

___ ___ ___ ___ ___ - ___ ___ ___

82¢ 41¢ 60¢ 75¢ 97¢ 39¢ 97¢ 97¢

Name: ______________________ Date: ____________

Riddle 36

How do you make any watch a stopwatch?

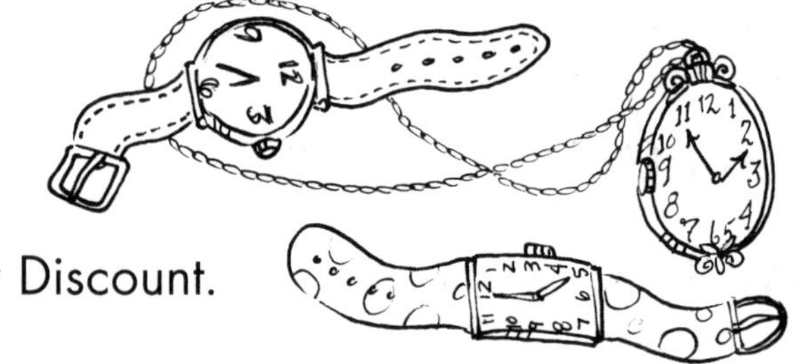

Add the cost of the items from Dan's Dollar Discount. Solve the riddle using your answers below.

Dan's Dollar Discount		
elephant eraser . . . . . 40¢ monkey magnet . . . . . 10¢	glitter putty . . . . 75¢ spinning top . . . . 15¢	kangaroo key chain . . 55¢ magic coin trick . . . . . 60¢

1 glitter putty and 1 monkey magnet cost ________¢ (W)	1 glitter putty and 2 monkey magnets cost ________¢ (O)
1 spinning top and 1 elephant eraser cost ________¢ (T)	3 spinning tops cost ________¢ (E)
1 magic coin trick and 1 elephant eraser cost $ ________ (D)	1 monkey magnet, 1 spinning top, and 1 kangaroo key chain cost ________¢ (N)
How many elephant erasers can you buy with $1.00? ________¢ (F)	How many monkey magnets can you buy with $1.00? ________¢ (I)

Solve the Riddle! Write the letter that goes with each number or value.

___ ___ ___ ' ___   ___ ___ ___ ___   ___ ___ .

$1.00 95¢ 80¢ 55¢   85¢ 10 80¢ $1.00   10 55¢

Name: ______________________ Date: ____________

Riddle 37

What kind of mail do fish get?

Add the coin values.
How much more do you need to make $1.00?
Solve the riddle using your answers below.

+ + ______¢ = $1.00 (C)
+ + ______¢ = $1.00 (D)
+ + ______¢ = $1.00 (O)
+ + ______¢ = $1.00 (T)
+ + ______¢ = $1.00 (S)
+ + + ______¢ = $1.00 (P)

Solve the Riddle! Write the letter that goes with each value.

____ ____ ____ ____   ____ ____ ____ ____
5¢ 45¢ 77¢ 85¢   15¢ 45¢ 35¢ 77¢

Name: ______________________ Date: ____________

Riddle 38

What kind of cake do chickens like to bake?

Make change from $1.00.
Solve the riddle using your answers below.

You spend 40¢. You have ______¢ left. M	You spend 65¢. You have ______¢ left. R
You spend 79¢. You have ______¢ left. A	You spend 85¢. You have ______¢ left. K
You spend 33¢. You have ______¢ left. S	You spend 90¢. You have ______¢ left. L
You spend 57¢. You have ______¢ left. Y	You spend 24¢. You have ______¢ left. I
You spend 48¢. You have ______¢ left. H	You spend 11¢. You have ______¢ left. B
You spend 8¢. You have ______¢ left. C	You spend 94¢. You have ______¢ left. E

Solve the Riddle! Write the letter that goes with each value.

___ ___ ___ - ___ ___ ___ ___ ___ ___
10¢ 21¢ 43¢ 6¢ 35¢ 92¢ 21¢ 15¢ 6¢

Name: ______________________ Date: ____________

Riddle 39

What's the best way to treat a baby goat?

Find the answers to the problems.
Solve the riddle using your answers below.

= ________¢
A

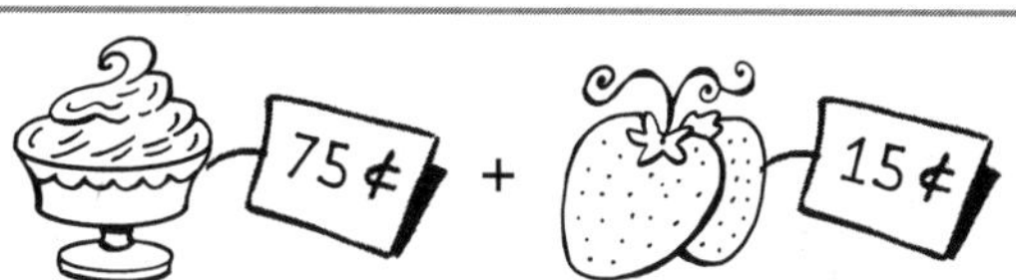

How much does this dessert cost? ______ ¢
E

What do you need to make $1.00?

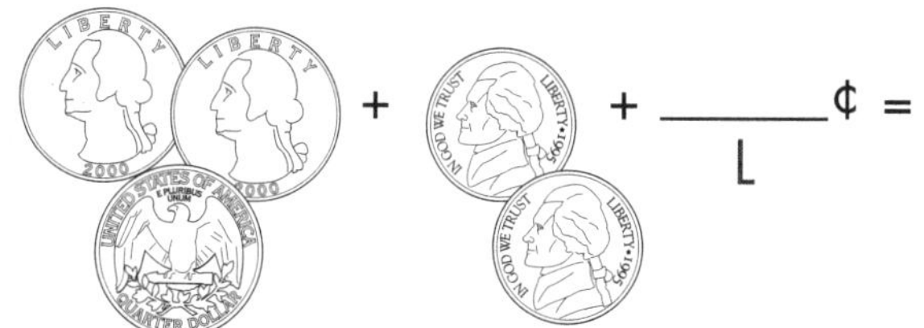

+ ______¢ =
L

You have $1.00.

You spend 67¢.

You have ________¢ left.
K

How much do 4 balloons cost?

$ ________
I

How many can you buy with $1.00? _______
D

Solve the Riddle! Write the letter that goes with each number or value.

___	___	___	___		___		___	___	___
15¢	$1.00	33¢	90¢		45¢		33¢	$1.00	3

Name: ______________________ Date: __________

Riddle 40

What's the best day to go to the beach?

Add the coin and dollar values.
Solve the riddle using your answers below.

$\$$______ N	$\$$______ D
$\$$______ A	$\$$______ S
$\$$______ U	$\$$______ Y

Solve the Riddle! Write the letter that goes with each value.

___ ___ ___ ___ ___ ___
$1.45 $1.26 $1.50 $1.57 $1.78 $1.29

Name: ____________________ Date: ____________

Riddle 41

What goes around the world but stays in a corner?

Add the cost of items from the menu.
Solve the riddle using your answers below.

The Ice Cream Scoop		
1 scoop . . . . 50¢ 2 scoops $1.00	3 scoops . . . . . $1.75 chocolate syrup . . 30¢	sprinkles . . . . 15¢ nuts . . . . 25¢

2 scoops with sprinkles cost $ ________ T	3 scoops with sprinkles cost $ ________ M
3 scoops with nuts cost $ ________ A	2 scoops with sprinkles and nuts cost $ ________ H
2 scoops with sprinkles and chocolate syrup cost $ ________ P	1 scoop with nuts, chocolate syrup, and sprinkles cost $ ________ S

Solve the Riddle! Write the letter that goes with each value.

___   ___ ___ ___ ___ ___

$2.00 $1.20 $1.15 $2.00 $1.90 $1.45

Name: ____________________ Date: __________

Riddle 42

What did one road say to the other road?

Add the coin and dollar values. How much more do you need to make $2.00? Solve the riddle using your answers below.

 + _____¢ = $2.00
A

 + _____¢ = $2.00
H

 + _____¢ = $2.00
I

 + _____¢ = $2.00
E

 + _____¢ = $2.00
W

+ _____¢ = $2.00
Y

Solve the Riddle! Write the letter that goes with each .

___ ___ , ___ ___ ___ !
80¢ 25¢ 97¢ 75¢ 89¢

Name: ____________________ Date: ____________

Riddle 43

Which knight wore tap shoes?

Make change from $2.00
Solve the riddle using your answers below.

You spend 25¢. You have $ ______ left. T	You spend 46¢. You have $ ______ left. C
You spend 58¢. You have $ ______ left. H	You spend 17¢. You have $ ______ left. S
You spend 22¢. You have $ ______ left. L	You spend 79¢. You have $ ______ left. D
You spend 92¢. You have $ ______ left. N	You spend 34¢. You have $ ______ left. I
You spend 10¢. You have $ ______ left. R	You spend 26¢. You have $ ______ left. O
You spend 49¢. You have $ ______ left. A	You spend 87¢. You have $ ______ left. E

Solve the Riddle! Write the letter that goes with each value.

___ ___ ___   ___ ___ ___ ___ ___ ___ ___ ___
$1.83 $1.66 $1.90 $1.21 $1.51 $1.08 $1.54 $1.13 $1.78 $1.74 $1.75

Name: ______________________ Date: ____________

Riddle 44

What do you call a chef who can't cook pancakes?

Find the answers to the problems.
Solve the riddle using your answers below.

    = $______ F	You have $2.00. You spend 39¢. You have $ ______ left. L
How much more do you need to make $2.00?  + $. ______ = O  	  How much do these cat toys cost $ ______ A
How many party hats can you buy with $2.00? ______ P 	  How much do 2 frames cost? $ ______ I

Solve the Riddle! Write the letter that goes with each number or value.

___		___	___	___	___	-	___	___	___	___
$1.80		$1.45	$1.61	$1.90	2		$1.45	$1.61	$.65	2

Name: ______________________ Date: ____________

Riddle 45

What do little gorillas learn first in school?

Add the coin and dollar values.
Solve the riddle using your answers below.

	$________ B
	$________ A
	$________ P
	$________ E
	$________ S
	$________ C

Solve the Riddle! Write the letter that goes with each value.

___ ___ ___ - ___ - ___ ' ___

$2.50 $4.62 $4.65 $2.80 $3.45 $4.05

Name: ____________________ Date: ____________

Riddle 46

What do sea monsters like to eat?

Add the cost of the items on the list.
Solve the riddle using your answers below.

School Supplies		
spiral notebook ...... $2.00 ring binder $3.50	3-hole paper .... $1.00 box of pencils $1.25	highlighter .... 60¢ eraser............... 20¢

2 spiral notebooks cost $ ________ H	3 erasers and 3-hole paper cost $ ________ D
1 ring binder and 3-hole paper cost $ ________ A	3-hole paper and 1 box of pencils cost $ ________ F
3-hole paper, 1 box of pencils, and 1 highlighter cost $ ________ P	1 spiral notebook, 1 eraser, and 1 highlighter cost $ ________ S
1 spiral notebook and 1 eraser cost $ ________ N	1 ring binder and 1 box of pencils cost $ ________ I

Solve the Riddle! Write the letter that goes with each value.

___ ___ ___ ___   ___ ___ ___
$2.25 $4.75 $2.80 $4.00 $4.50 $2.20 $1.60

___ ___ ___ ___ ___
$2.80 $4.00 $4.75 $2.85 $2.80

Name: ______________________ Date: ____________

Riddle 47

How can you hold water in a sieve?

Add the money values. How much more do you need to make $5.00? Solve the riddle using your answers below.

Money	Missing amount	Total
	+ $ ________ (R)	= $5.00
	+ $ ________ (Z)	= $5.00
	+ $ ________ (I)	= $5.00
	+ $ ________ (E)	= $5.00
	+ $ ________ (T)	= $5.00
	+ $ ________ (F)	= $5.00

Solve the Riddle! Write the letter that goes with each value.

___ ___ ___ ___ ___ ___   ___ ___ .
$3.97 $1.85 $2.90 $2.90 $1.25 $2.90 $2.60 $1.50

Name: ______________________ Date: ____________

Riddle 48

Why did the mother parrot scold her baby?

Make change from $5.00. Solve the riddle using your answers below.

You spend 76¢. You have $ ________ left. T	You spend 98¢. You have $ ________ left. K
You spend $2.39. You have $ ________ left. H	You spend $2.17. You have $ ________ left. C
You spend $3.62. You have $ ________ left. L	You spend $1.49. You have $ ________ left. D
You spend $3.35. You have $ ________ left. N	You spend 56¢. You have $ ________ left. I
You spend $2.85. You have $ ________ left. R	You spend $4.73. You have $. ________ left. B
You spend $1.83. You have $ ________ left. A	You spend $2.99. You have $ ________ left. E

Solve the Riddle! Write the letter that goes with each value.

___ ___   ___ ___ ___ ___ ' ___
$2.61 $2.01 $3.51 $4.44 $3.51 $1.65 $4.24

___ ___ ___ ___   ___ ___ ___ ___ .
$4.24 $3.17 $1.38 $4.02 $.27 $3.17 $2.83 $4.02

Name: ____________________ Date: ____________

Riddle 49

What animals drop from the sky?

Find the answers to the problems.
Solve the riddle using your answers below.

= $ ________
I

You have $5.00.

You spend $1.82.

You have $ ________ left.
D

How much more do you need to make $5.00?

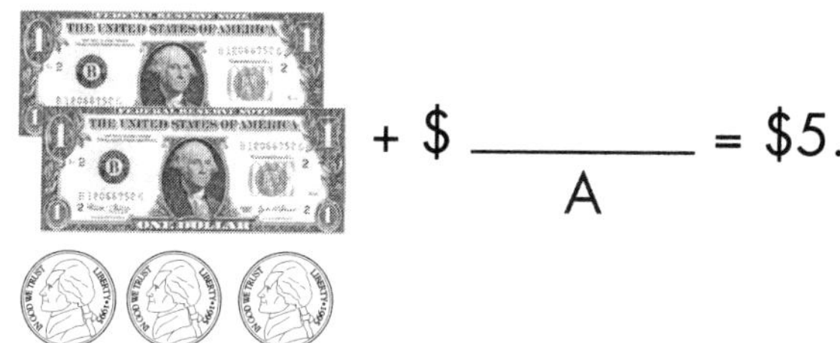

+ $ ________ = $5.00
A

How much do these items cost?

$ ________
R

How many soft pretzels can you buy with $5.00? ________
E

How much do 3 toy cars cost?

$ ________
N

Solve the Riddle! Write the letter that goes with each number or value.

___	___	___	___	–	___	___	___	___
$4.00	$2.85	$4.80	$4.95		$3.18	5	5	$4.00

Name: ______________________ Date: ______________

Riddle 50

How much is a skunk worth?

Add the coin and dollar values.
Solve the riddle using your answers below.

$ ________ O

$ ________ E

$ ________ T

$ ________ C

$ ________ S

$ ________ N

Solve the Riddle! Write the letter that goes with each value.

___ ___ ___   ___ ___ ___ ___ ___
$7.75 $8.08 $7.53 $6.50 $9.75 $7.53 $8.08 $5.25

Name: ______________________ Date: ____________

Riddle 51

What game do hogs like best?

Add to find out how much lunch costs.
Solve the riddle using your answers below.

Dina's Diner Menu		
SANDWICHES	SALADS	DRINKS
Tuna $6.25	Small salad $2.75	Milk $1.75
Turkey $5.50	Large salad $3.75	Smoothie $3.25
Grilled cheese $4.25	Sliced tomato $1.75	Juice $2.50

Grilled cheese and milk cost $ ________ D	Tuna sandwich and a small salad cost $ ________ N
Turkey sandwich and a large salad cost $ ________ Y	Large salad with sliced tomato costs $ ________ P
Tuna sandwich and a smoothie cost $ ________ A	Smoothie and a large salad cost $ ________ O
Turkey sandwich and milk cost $ ________ I	Grilled cheese and juice cost $ ________ G

Solve the Riddle! Write the letter that goes with each value.

___ ___ ___ – ___ ___ ___ ___
$5.50 $7.25 $6.75 $5.50 $7.00 $9.00 $6.75

Name: ____________________ Date: ____________

Riddle 52

What does a mother seagull sing at bedtime?

Add the coin and dollar values. How much more do you need to make $10.00? Solve the riddle using your answers below.

+ $ ________ = $10.00
U

+ $ ________ = $10.00
Y

+ $ ________ = $10.00
L

+ $ ________ = $10.00
A

+ $ ________ = $10.00
G

+ $ ________ = $10.00
B

Solve the Riddle! Write the letter that goes with each value.

___		___	___	___	___	-	___	-	___	___
$5.80		$4.96	$6.85	$3.00	$3.00		$5.80		$7.50	$4.75

Name: ____________________ Date: ____________

Riddle 53

How do baby fish know how to swim?

Add the cost of the items. Then figure the change you will get. Solve the riddle using your answers below.

Artie's Art Shop	
box of crayons . . . . $1.50 set of colored pencils $1.75	set of markers . . . . $2.25 sketch pad $4.00

2 boxes of crayons cost $ ________. I Your change from $10.00 is $ ________. N	1 sketch pad and 1 set of markers cost $ ________. T Your change from $10.00 is $ ________. F
1 box of crayons and 1 set of colored pencils cost $ ________. L Your change from $10.00 is $ ________. B	2 sets of markers cost $ ________. S Your change from $10.00 is $ ________. C

Solve the Riddle! Write the letter that goes with each value.

___ ___ ___ – ___ ___ ___ ___ ___ ___

$3.75 $3.00 $7.00 $4.50 $6.25 $3.00 $7.00 $5.50 $6.25

Name: ______________________ Date: ____________

Riddle 54

What does the magician say when he takes a picture?

Find the answers to the problems.
Solve the riddle using your answers below.

= $ ____________ S

You have $10.00.

You spend $.44.

You have $ ____________ left. C

How much more do you need to make $10.00?

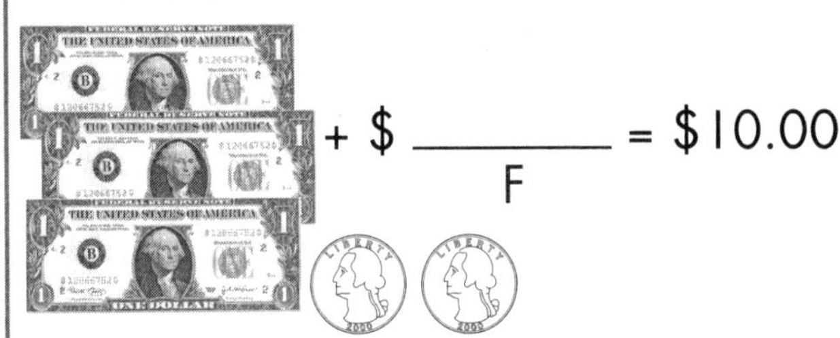

+ $ ____________ = $10.00
F

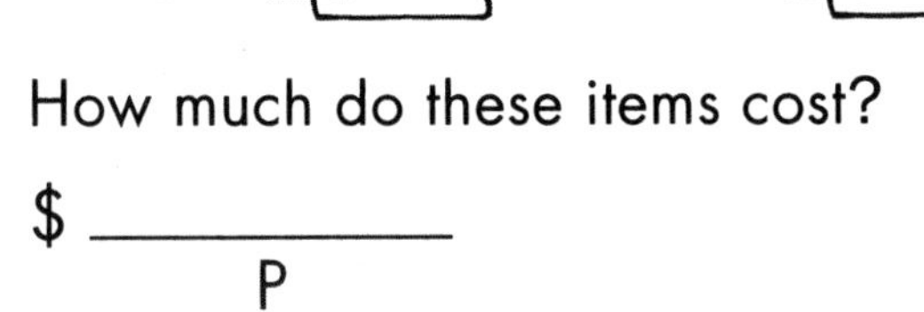

How much do these items cost?

$ ____________ P

How many yo-yos can you buy with $10.00? ____________ U

How much do 2 model planes cost?

$ ____________ O

Solve the Riddle! Write the letter that goes with each number or value.

___	___	___	___	___	-	___	___	___	___	___
$6.50	$9.90	$9.56	3	$7.45		$5.35	$9.90	$9.56	3	$7.45

Name: ______________________ Date: ____________

What is the opposite of a restaurant?

About how much does each item cost?
Circle the best estimate. Solve the riddle using your answers below.

(sneakers)	$20.00 R	$2.00 V	$.20 S	(banana)	$50.00 B	$5.00 I	$.50 A
(T-shirt)	$10.00 W	$1.00 M	$.10 P	(pizza slice)	$25.00 C	$2.50 K	$.25 G
(paint set)	$30.00 F	$3.00 T	$.30 Y	(GLUE stick)	$7.00 J	$.70 O	$.07 L
(burger, fries, drink)	$40.00 D	$4.00 E	$.40 Z	(SPACE Puppy! DVD)	$15.00 N	$1.50 H	$.15 U

Solve the Riddle! Write the letter that goes with each value.

___ $.50

___ $10.00 ___ $.70 ___ $20.00 ___ $2.50 ___ $4.00 ___ $20.00 – ___ $.50 ___ $15.00 ___ $3.00

Name: ______________________ Date: __________

Riddle 56

Where do kittens go shopping?

About how much does each item cost?
Round each price to the nearest dollar.
Circle the closest estimate.
Solve the riddle using your answers below.

Item	Choice 1	Choice 2	Choice 3	Item	Choice 1	Choice 2	Choice 3
Popcorn, $1.89 each	$1.00 R	$2.00 A	$3.00 X	Clock (4:15), $6.79 each	$5.00 L	$6.00 B	$7.00 O
Flag, 99¢ each	$1.00 N	$2.00 Y	$3.00 H	Doll, $4.99 each	$4.00 E	$5.00 G	$6.00 J
Marbles, $2.69 each	$2.00 K	$3.00 C	$4.00 Z	Headphones, $8.29	$7.00 D	$8.00 I	$9.00 M
Fire truck (LADDER 5), $6.19 each	$5.00 Q	$6.00 L	$7.00 V	Book, $4.39 each	$4.00 T	$5.00 S	$6.00 P

Solve the Riddle! Write the letter that goes with each value.

___ ___   ___
$8.00 $1.00 $2.00

___ ___ ___ - ___ ___ ___ ___
$3.00 $2.00 $4.00 - $2.00 $6.00 $7.00 $5.00

Name: ____________________ Date: ____________

Riddle 57

What bird is with you at every meal?

Circle the best estimate.
Solve the riddle using your answers below.

<table>
<tr>
<td>

About how much do both items cost?

$6.00	$7.00	$8.00
P	H	S

</td>
<td>

About how much do 3 pounds of apples cost?

$1.00	$2.00	$3.00
N	L	F

</td>
</tr>
<tr>
<td>

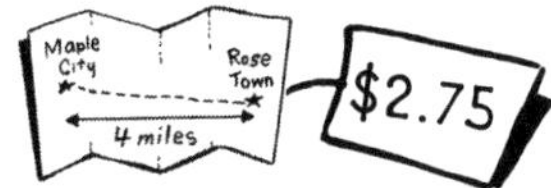

About how much do a map and a pair of hiking books cost?

$12.00	$13.00	$14.00
E	O	T

</td>
<td>

About how much does a taco and juice cost?

$6.00	$7.00	$8.00
B	A	M

</td>
</tr>
<tr>
<td>

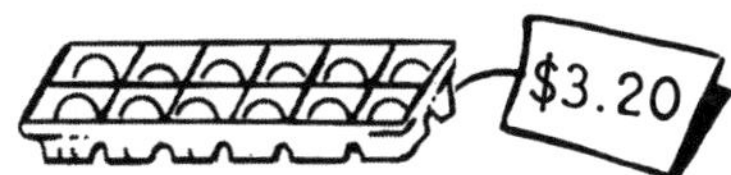

About how much do 3 dozen eggs cost?

$10.00	$11.00	$12.00
W	C	R

</td>
<td>

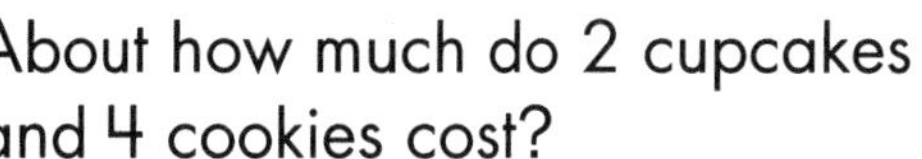

About how much do 2 cupcakes and 4 cookies cost?

$3.00	$4.00	$5.00
D	K	I

</td>
</tr>
</table>

Solve the Riddle! Write the letter that goes with each value.

___		___	___	___	___	___	___	___
$7.00		$8.00	$10.00	$7.00	$2.00	$2.00	$13.00	$10.00

Answer Key

page 5: Riddle 1
a fire alarm
L-5:00, D-7:00, F-10:00, E-11:00, I-2:00, M-8:00, R-6:00, A-9:00, B-1:00

page 6: Riddle 2
Croaker Jacks
O-4:30, B-8:30, A-2:30, K-6:30, E-9:30, C-7:30, J-1:30, R-12:30, S-3:30

page 7: Riddle 3
Mars-mallows
A-2:15, B-8:45, M-1:15, R-6:45, L-10:15, O-4:45, W-9:15, S-12:45, E-3:15

page 8: Riddle 4
a bully goat
L-1:30, B-9:00, G-3:30, T-6:00, A-10:15, U-1:15, O-2:30, Y-12:45, R-3:15

page 9: Riddle 5
fur-ious
S-3:20, U-7:40, E-2:40, F-1:40, A-8:20, I-4:20, R-9:20, T-10:20, O-12:40

page 10: Riddle 6
fire flies
L-9:10, E-5:20, H-1:50, N-3:50, F-7:40, S-11:10, R-4:10, T-2:50, I-10:40

page 11: Riddle 7
ow-wow!
O-5:05, F-7:10, T-11:35, S-2:25, L-6:55, E-8:05, N-6:15, W-10:45, I-4:25

page 12: Riddle 8
Puppet Chow
C-2:25, P-10:35, U-7:05, W-8:10, F-8:25, T-5:50, H-4:50, E-3:20, O-9:40

page 13: Riddle 9
Look before you creep.
B-12:00, K-11:00, F-2:00, Y-5:00, S-3:00, L-9:00, R-7:00, C-4:00, O-8:00, U-1:00, P-10:00, E-6:00

page 14: Riddle 10
hive and seek
A-2:30, H-2:00, N-5:30, I-6:30, S-12:00, E-1:30, V-12:30, B-7:30, F-3:00, D-10:30, R-9:00, K-11:00

page 15: Riddle 11
tweet-hearts
D-1:15, N-1:00, E-1:30, H-7:45, R-7:30, V-8:00, W-4:45, M-4:30, S-5:00, N-10:15, T-10:00, A-10:30

page 16: Riddle 12
the winner
E-1:30, N-1:00, D-1:45, I-9:30, L-8:30, W-11:30, T-7:30, U-6:30, R-8:00, S-3:30, H-3:15, M-6:00

page 17: Riddle 13
They tide.
E-1:20, T-1:00, L-1:40, P-7:00, C-6:40, I-7:20, A-4:30, D-4:10, Y-4:50, M-11:40, H-11:20, J-12:00

page 18: Riddle 14
Push it.
H-2:40, A-2:30, U-2:50, W-8:30, P-8:20, E-8:40, T-5:10, F-5:00, I-5:20, S-10:50, R-10:40, N-11:00

page 19: Riddle 15
Howl-oween
E-1:30, W-1:25, T-1:35, A-9:20, H-9:15, S-9:25, J-6:10, O-6:05, C-6:15, N-11:15, R-11:10, L-11:20

page 20: Riddle 16
a cupcake
U-2:30, G-2:10, B-2:35, C-3:00, N-2:55, E-3:10, A-8:30, W-8:20, P-8:40, K-12:20, R-12:10, I-12:30

page 21: Riddle 17
an unfair-y tale
A-4:05, U-11:40, Y-1:45, I-6:35, F-9:10, R-2:45, T-5:40, D-7:40, S-1:30, E-4:30, L-2:55, N-12:45

page 22: Riddle 18
eleph-ant
A-6:45, P-7:50, R-3:30, E-11:05, T-9:15, N-2:45, L-5:40, H-12:45, S-1:15, W-4:35

page 23: Riddle 19
oak-meal
A-7:15 AM, M-3:30 PM, N-5:00 PM, E-12:10 PM, O-5:45 AM, L-7:00 AM, T-8:30 PM, K-9:10 AM

page 24: Riddle 20
Cop Sticks
P-12:30 PM, F-3:45 AM, N-9:10 AM, C-1:40 AM, T-11:15 AM, I-3:45 PM, O-9:10 PM, B-12:30 AM, K-1:40 PM, S-11:15 PM

page 25: Riddle 21
the letter L
P-7:50, T-2:55, E-4:15, O-5:30, F-6:20, A-12:30, H-1:00 PM, D-4:30 AM, R-3:30 PM, L-7:15 AM

page 26: Riddle 22
kook-atoos
B-120, O-60, R-65, S-40, A-90, J-30, E-140, K-15, T-100, Y-10

page 27: Riddle 23
crazy!
Z-80, E-120, D-130, R-30, Y-100, M-90, C-10, L-75, O-45, A-50

page 28: Riddle 24
biscuit ball
U-7, B-10, A-30, S-4, I-12, L-28, C-15, T-25

page 29: Riddle 25
a rude-eo
D-9:15, A-45, O-30, U-15, R-11:00, E-60

page 30: Riddle 26
I lava you.
A-30, L-28, Y-3, E-24, I-5, V-17, O-11, U-19

page 31: Riddle 27
Moo-souri
O-5, S-8, P-14, I-25, A-11, M-23, R-18, U-29

page 32: Riddle 28
steel
E-62, T-61, R-60, I-92, S-58, O-91, N-59, L-93

page 33: Riddle 29
bee-kinis
B-48, N-26, S-12, I-104, K-14, E-6, M-21, T-24

page 34: Riddle 30
envelope
L-6¢, V-35¢, E-15¢, P-30¢, O-11¢, N-50¢

page 35: Riddle 31
sting beans
B-24. T-28¢, I-40¢, G-50¢, S-36¢, E-33¢, A-2, N-3

page 36: Riddle 32
tutu-lips
U-15¢, I-25¢, S-20¢, R-35¢, L-10¢, P-5¢, O-30¢, T-40¢

page 37: Riddle 33
two feet
O-10¢, R-39¢, E-11¢, W-27¢, K-35¢, L-40¢, Y-23¢, F-16¢, H-2¢, B-33¢, T-43¢, J-19¢

page 38: Riddle 34
well water
E-25¢, P-36¢, T-46¢, H-18¢, A-20¢, W-15¢, L-45¢, R-5¢

page 39: Riddle 35
tango-roo
A-41¢, O-97¢, R-39¢, N-60¢, G-75¢, T-82¢

page 40: Riddle 36
Don't wind it.
W-85¢, O-95¢, T-55¢, E-45¢, D-$1.00, N-80¢, F-2, I-10

page 41: Riddle 37
post cods
C-15¢, D-35¢, O-45¢, T-85¢, S-77¢, P-5¢

page 42: Riddle 38
lay-er cake
M-60¢, R-35¢, A-21¢, K-15¢, S-67¢, L-10¢, Y-43¢, I-76¢, H-52¢, B-89¢, C-92¢, E-6¢

page 43: Riddle 39
like a kid
A-45¢, E-90¢, L-15¢, K-33¢, I-$1.00, D-3

Answer Key

page 44: Riddle 40
Sunday
N-$1.50, D-$1.57, A-$1.78, S-$1.45, U-$1.26, Y-$1.29

page 45: Riddle 41
a stamp
T-$1.15, M-$1.90, A-$2.00, H-$2.40, P-$1.45, S-$1.20

page 46: Riddle 42
Hi, way!
A-75¢, H-80¢, I-25¢, E-50¢, W-97¢, Y-89¢

page 47: Riddle 43
Sir Dancelot
T-$1.75, C-$1.54, H-$1.42, S-$1.83, L-$1.78, D-$1.21, N-$1.08, I-$1.66, R-$1.90, O-$1.74, A-$1.51, E-$1.13

page 48: Riddle 44
a flip-flop
F-$1.45, L-$1.61, O-$.65, A-$1.80, P-2, I-$1.90

page 49: Riddle 45
APE-B-C's
B-$2.80, A-$2.50, P-$4.62, E-$4.65, S-$4.05, C-$3.45

page 50: Riddle 46
fish and ships
H-$4.00, D-$1.60, A-$4.50, F-$2.25, P-$2.85, S-$2.80, N-$2.20, I-$4.75

page 51: Riddle 47
Freeze it.
R-$1.85, Z-$1.25, I-$2.60, E-$2.90, T-$1.50, F-$3.97

page 52: Riddle 48
He didn't talk back.
T-$4.24, K-$4.02, H-$2.61, C-$2.83, L-$1.38, D-$3.51, N-$1.65, I-$4.44, R-$2.15, B-$.27, A-$3.17, E-$2.01

page 53: Riddle 49
rain-deer
I-$4.80, D-$3.18, A-$2.85, R-$4.00, E-5, N-$4.95

page 54: Riddle 50
one scent
O-$7.75, E -$7.53, T-$5.25, C-$9.75, S-$6.50, N-$8.08

page 55: Riddle 51
pig-pong
D-$6.00, N-$9.00, Y-$9.25, P-$5.50, A-$9.50, O-$7.00, I-$7.25, G-$6.75

page 56: Riddle 52
a gull-a-by
U-$6.85, Y-$4.75, L-$3.00, A-$5.80, G-$4.96, B-$7.50

page 57: Riddle 53
fin-stinct
I-$3.00, N-$7.00, T-$6.25, F-$3.75, L-$3.25, B-$6.75, S-$4.50, C-$5.50

page 58: Riddle 54
focus-pocus
S-$7.45, C-$9.56, F-$6.50, P-$5.35, U-3, O-$9.90

page 59: Riddle 55
a worker-ant
R-$20.00, A-$.50, W-$10.00, K-$2.50, T-$3.00, O-$.70, E-$4.00, N-$15.00

page 60: Riddle 56
in a cat-alog
A-$2.00, O-$7.00, N-$1.00, G-$5.00, C-$3.00, I-$8.00, L-$6.00, T-$4.00

page 61: Riddle 57
a swallow
S-$8.00, L-$2.00, O-$13.00, A-$7.00, W-$10.00, K-$4.00